Dorothea Westhofen-Kunz

Stars
of Heaven
as
Messengers
of Love

AF191880

Volume 1

In deep empathy
with my friends
in the visible and invisible world

Bibliographical information
of Deutsche Nationalbibliothek

Deutsche Nationalbibliothek lists
this publication in the German national bibliography;
detailed bibliographical data
are obtainable online via dnb.d-nb.de

Copyright © Dorothea Westhofen-Kunz, 2012
First Edition 2012
ISBN 9783842356887
Printed in Germany
Manufactured and published by
Books on Demand GmbH, Norderstedt, Germany

Content

Preface

This book is dedicated to all of us, who through our divine mission, bring light into this world and who are constantly striving towards experiencing and sharing the eternal love of our Creator.

Those of us who hear this calling are called Stars of Heaven.

Just as the stars illuminate the heavens, so we radiate through the love of God and illuminate the darkness for all people who are helplessly in search of the light.

> *If it is possible for you*
> *to enrich with only one spark*
> *the love in this world,*
> *then you have not lived in vain.*
>
> *(Jack London)*

We have been sent by God to help people learn that they must help each other and to practice compassion at all times, for ourselves and for all those we meet on our life's journey. It is our mission to guide people back to the love of God; our hearts must meet in love.

Humanity seems not to hear the abundance of spiritual guidance and support that is available to us, for this reason we need to be aware and actively involve ourselves in guidance which finds us in quiet moments, in busy streets, in our sleep and in our waking.

In the course of this listening, we should not be overly modest and reserved but we should instead press on with courage and lead by example. We are always available to others with determination and infinite patience, but in an expression of love for ourselves, we sometimes need to be steadfast and rigorous.

It is mercy
that we may act as Stars of Heaven.

We can completely entrust our lives to God and we are therefore obliged to function through His love. Keeping this in mind, we always have to ascertain and question those areas and concerns that influence us from moment to moment. Sometimes, due to our uniqueness and positioning in the universe we are expected to be relatively inconspicuous, and in this situation, humility and under-statement is required. We must believe that the message we bring will float in the hearts of those we bring it to and we must learn to trust that the message will land, even if we are not there to see it. We must trust the message and trust ourselves as the messenger.

Concentrate on the task and
work on your self-improvement!

As a star of heaven open-mindedness is required. This is the primary objective in order to succeed in our mission. There is no other way, as the renewed conversion through God's spirit according to Luke, 17, 19 says:

Your faith will save you!

It is easily said: 'Your faith will save you', but are we really aware of the significance of this statement? The following example will shed some light on this.

My friend J. came over for a visit with her children, we drank coffee on our terrace. Her four-year-old daughter and our son were playing in the garden which was a level lower; her 18 month old son was playing around us. Suddenly we heard the small boy crying miserably. Startled, we all jumped up. With horror we saw that he had fallen from a height of four meters through a previously undiscovered hole in the terrace railing and he was now lying prostrate on the lawn. I picked up the child, called my husband and placed the boy on the sofa in the living-room, where I usually occupy myself with my Star of Heaven work. My husband examined the boy for bone fractures and I turned to my friend and asked the question: 'Do you believe?' At first she started fumbling uncomfortably and then she straightened her shoulders and looked deep into my eyes and said: 'Yes, I believe'. Only now, I could ask for her son to be healed. We gave her a cup of tea to calm her nerves and after an hour, she left for home with her kids. When I called her the next morning she confirmed what I had already known; her son had survived the fall unharmed.

What does it mean to be a Messenger of Love?

To be a Messenger of Love is part of the multiple functions that we must undertake in being Stars of Heaven.

Sometimes our function is comparable to that of an Angel, other times we seem to be like crystals embedded in dark rock, illuminating clarity and purity into the world. Alternatively, at times we undertake our divine mission with a revolutionary fighting spirit as guardians and protectors of God's love and creation.

We send love.

Stars of Heaven are God's helpers; we live completely in His love and carry out His Divine will. All emotions are known to us, but we must vibrate at the highest frequencies of love and make these other emotions guides that share our practices and compassion. We try to make all emotions except love foreign to us, even as we love them for bringing us their wisdom of being human. God is always central to what we do.

The true meaning of life
is the elevation of the soul.

It is our mission to keep our energy high and positive with unshakeable faith. Our Divine work is to free people from their negative and maladaptive emotions and guide their souls back to God's love. We restore faith in God and we help humanity to help themselves.

Our function is only effective within
the boundaries of a person's free will.

Every person decides for him- or herself, whether to make use of this inexhaustible blessing, as it is available for everyone who turns to us for help. We serve as a place of refuge and salvation for mankind. We may not leave anyone behind and we may also not just give up on someone, if we find the work too hard or too over-bearing.

It is grace to serve God as a Star of Heaven.

We work under the complete blessing of God. We should nevertheless always be aware that this blessing is uncontrollable and unpredictable. We are committed to carry out the Message of Love at any time and in any place. It is not up to us to judge other people or to decide what their spiritual learning has to be, we simply present ourselves wrapped in love and grace to shine our light on them. Sometimes this is silent, sometimes there are words, sometimes there is a look. However, there is always an energy that passes between the density of our humanity which reaches into the very fabric of our combined Divinity.

Priorities as a Star of Heaven

We must be fully committed to our mission. We should be prepared to change our internal and external lifestyle at any time and in any way until the Message of Love is completely integrated into our day-to-day existence. Nonetheless, it happens repeatedly that we find ourselves competing with the conflicting interests of ordinary and everyday life. Therefore, it is vital never to lose sight of our goal.

Almost everyone is familiar with the following situation: There are documents that need to be prepared for the next day's meeting. At the same time a dinner invitation at a friend's house crops up and on the same evening a work-group for Stars of Heaven is taking place and on top of that a child gets sick or another family member needs our help.

The following list serves as a guideline on how to align our priorities correctly:

- Above all is God, as we honour of His presence and His all-encompassing love towards us, as well as our trust in Him.

- Our immediate family is next. When we live with integrity and have created or restored balance within our family dynamics, only then are we allowed to work on other things within the framework as a Messenger of Love.

- After that we may start with our missions as Stars of Heaven.

- Earthly work and friends are next in line. Nevertheless, it is always pointed out that we should continue to pursue our day-to-day work and responsibilities. The Apostle Paul can serve as a reference, who worked as a tent-maker (see Apostles, 18, 3).

- Other people like neighbours, acquaintances and colleagues have the next priority.

The dilemma from the previous example can be solved with the help of these guidelines. If such an evening presents itself to you, take care of the child or family member, skip the dinner and leave the work for Stars of Heaven and the documents for later.

We always have enough time!

In general, as a Star of Heaven we should always have sufficient time. Our spirits and bodies are being watched and all obstacles are cleared out of the way, when the work is Divine work.

Nevertheless, we may from time to time feel overwhelmed, especially when certain areas of our lives and people who are close to us and towards whom we feel obliged, demand our complete and utter attention.

Here it is very clear to distinguish, whether we are given a respite from working as a Star of Heaven, so that we can recharge our batteries again, or if the circumstances are purposefully orchestrated, in order for us to let go and escape from earthly matters.

In the case of earthly matters, it is up to us to decide, how far and how deep we are willing to engage ourselves to delve into the situation at hand. Especially here, the communication using the method of *Bridging* can act as an important decision making aid (see chapter 'Bridging and Active Listening').

As a result, we notice once again that our daily tasks are far less important than our divine mission and in many cases their urgency is taken away from us as we do our work for God.

If we feel overwhelmed with our divine work as a Star of Heaven, we may here again use Bridging to find out whether or not we are on the right track.

We could also solve our aforementioned challenges differently, depending on what information we receive from our Spiritual Friends. There is the possibility that the child or family member can be taken care of by someone else and we can then direct our attention to the documents or the Stars of Heaven workgroup and we could also enjoy the dinner with friends. God does want us to have every opportunity to enjoy his creation, and all we have to do is to live in the moment, increase our vibrational frequency towards love and all that we need to achieve and experience can be ours in a moment.

The cases mentioned previously show us, that we cannot exhaust our decision making options through our connection with God often enough. All we have to do is ask and we can receive so much more support.

If we integrate communication with God more into our lives, then we will find our true selves. If we follow God's will and fulfil the tasks that are given to us as a Star of Heaven we will get a new perception and we will lack for nothing.

Over and above this, we should try to have as much contact with people as possible, so that God's glory befalls them (according to Acts, 5, 15). This means, that we should only dwell amongst large groups of people and strangers if we are requested to do so by our Spiritual Friends, like for example participating at an event or visiting public places.

Bridging and Active Listening

Gospel of John, 1, 1:

'In the beginning was the Word, and the Word was with God, and the Word was God.'

As Stars of Heaven, we get amazing support where we can really listen to our inner voice and hear the guidance of God. If our souls rest with God, nothing seems impossible.

Every religious believer is already familiar with the method of praying since childhood. Through prayer, we often turn help seeking to God pleading for support or advice. Only a few people are given the gift and ability to receive messages directly.

The Stars of Heaven have, beyond prayer, an additional very important communication method at their disposal. We call this method 'Bridging'. When communicating via Bridging, an applied psycho-kinesiological method is used to communicate with our Spiritual Friends. This communication takes place from both sides. Firstly, words of caution and requests, encouragement and consolation as well as tips and information are communicated through Bridging to the Stars of Heaven. Thereafter we receive the permission to express and ask questions by using Bridging.

First and foremost one of the most important steps is to master *Active Listening* with the help of the Bridging method. This can only be accomplished through the offered seminars, which are facilitated by persons who are experienced and have mastered this method. It is also described in detail in Volume 2, the workbook which accompanies the seminars.

We can always provide advice.

The help from our Spiritual Friends is limitless and at our infinite disposal. We should use it more and act on it as is destined for us. With the right connection, we receive scope to function freely and always know which direction to take.

Is work as a Star of Heaven for everyone?

The Stars of Heaven are chosen.

We are repeatedly asked to devote ourselves to the call as a Star of Heaven and to act as Messengers of Love. Should we decide to accept this call and follow this lesser trodden path, then our 'membership' of the community of Stars of Heaven shows itself in our fulfillment as living as Messengers of Love and through reaching our desired goals and dreams through a journey of unconditional love.

For a long time I searched for my roots and the meaning of my life. This lifelong search led me as a young adult to a monastery to find out whether I wanted to become a nun. In the following years, I scoured through the world religions and a great deal of spiritual belief systems. Only when I encountered people who introduced me to the Bridging method and its areas of influence and functions, did I know that I had finally found my purpose. Today I am very grateful having discovered my work as a Star of Heaven and to be able to share this process with people from all over the planet.

Stars of Heaven allow themselves to be guided through life by their Spiritual Friends. We agree to dissolve our old thinking patterns and bad habits. With this, we release ourselves from any kind of strange influences. With the support of our Spiritual Friends we improve the quality of how we listen to ourselves, our inner voice, the Divine voice within.

Furthermore, we undergo far-reaching internal changes, in order for God to make use of our essence, our talents and courage for us to be placed in positions of healing. All our skills and opportunities are developed in order to serve and to avail ourselves to the Divine work sent to us by our Creator.

We experience a complete change, a replacement of our self, see the letter to the Philippians, 3, 7:

"But whatever were gains to me, I now consider loss for the sake of Christ."

This process can both be lengthy and painful. We are tested through sweat and tears to see whether we are steadfast and firm; so to speak, to separate the husk from the corn. Nevertheless, we always undergo a transformation process and accept the risks, in order to live a comfortable and wonderful life.

Systematically we are freed from our emotional burdens until our consciousness is effectively changed so that we are filled with God's love. In this way we are able to wonderfully approach and transform other human beings, should they want to be transformed.

Besides the willingness to completely engage with God, there are three more character traits that describe the Stars of Heaven:

A strong belief;
A high degree of integrity;
Steadfastness during the storms of life.

It is very important to know, that we are not alone on the way to freedom and realization. With Bridging, our Spiritual Friends are by our side, accompanying us through our day-to-day lives. The author offers assistance in the form of seminars and workgroups to teach how to gain access and make use of Bridging (see imprint).

The concept of time whilst working as Messenger of Love

Often our desire to receive timely forecasts with Bridging is overpowering. Our concept of time is completely foreign to our Spiritual Friends. That is why it is difficult, almost impossible, to get reliable time indications of when things may happen.

The differentiation between the work as Messenger of Love and other practices

A clear differentiation between the work as a Messenger of Love and various other esoteric practices is essential. In order to find the right way of working as a Star of Heaven, we must be clear about the appropriateness of every new practice and every new method we are made aware of.

Some methods come from the fields of magic, PSI-Occult, Spiritualism and Fortune-telling and it is important that these may never be used in our Divine work.

To facilitate our work as Stars of Heaven we may however, from time to time use practices that gain us more insight into the case or that draws us into a particular situation. This is always explicitly communicated to us by our Spiritual Friends and so we must listen deeply before we engage in any practice or act of healing.

In contrast to other esoteric methods, we receive, as Messengers of Love, continuous help in our day-to-day lives and we are able to resolve emotions and clarify problematic situations without recourse to dangerous practices whose power we do not understand and that we cannot embody from a place of light.

Many people would really like to find out about their future. However, some people are already so addicted that they periodically search for advice and help from astrologers and people who read cards to deliver interpretations on the same subject. If it has been foretold that there are challenging and difficult times ahead, they demand answers from various astrologers and card readers in the hope of receiving a different answer and thus be able to change the future. This is not only based on curiosity but also rather on a non-avowed fear of life. When dealing with such a person we could, with the help of astrology and cards, uncover and interpret the subject matter at hand. We could of course just as well solve this depiction using Bridging.

As our function as Stars of Heaven comes to the fore, we may in this case ask for healing for the afflicted person. He or she will then be freed from the emotional burdens, which led to the dependency on astrology and card-reading in the first place.

Our Spiritual Friends

Spiritual Friends stand ready to accompany any Star of Heaven on their journey to accomplish their tasks ahead as well as tackling certain topics and situations which may arise.

The list of Spiritual Friends differs from country to country, from culture to culture and from belief system to belief system and this list of friends can be extended according to the circumstances necessitating their inclusion in the Divine work.

The complete list can be found in the workbook and will be shared during workshops.

Divine Accompanying Words

Since our work as Stars of Heaven and our mission as a Messenger of Love is sometimes quite challenging and demanding, this book contains supportive words of encouragement and consolation as well as words of caution and inspiration that any Star of Heaven can depend on and be inspired by.

'The rest of mankind who were not killed by these plagues still did not repent of the work of their hands; they did not stop worshiping demons, and idols of gold, silver, bronze, stone and wood-idols that cannot see or hear or walk. Nor did they repent of their murders, their magic arts, their sexual immorality or their thefts.' (Revelation, 9, 20-21)

Against this background, our work as Stars of Heaven is extremely important.

Overcome your fear!

Think positive thoughts, lead positive conversations, do positive things and surround yourself with positive people.

Forgive all those who are not like that, because they do not know any different.

You are
fishers
of
men

We
are allowed
to know
everything

*We
have access
to the
greatest secrets*

Always remember
the key message
of the Huna Science:
Never hurt,
just help

*Keep
your
strength
concealed*

*Stay far away
from community-clubs
and
secret societies*

Take on
the work
of
Jesus

Give
true testimony
of
God's work

Your soul
shall become
like
the calm sea

Time
is always right
for the right
deed

A time
will come
when nothing is
left anymore

You
shall see the world
through pink glasses and
act wholeheartedly
with the carefree
spirit of a child

Rejoice
in the Lord
all
the time

Live
with
the flow
of life

The
Lord
is near

Words of Divine Guidance

Stop wanting to pull the strings. Fulfil God's will only and accept His guidance. When doing this, you will become confident and secure.

Do not depend too much on your free will and do not play manipulative games.

The unbiased acceptance of the Divine is required.

Because… now He invisibly reigns and rules over the heavens, but the time will come when everything will be renewed. About this He always spoke through His prophets (according to Acts, 3, 21).

*Let yourself
be guided
every day
in a special way*

Never again
you will suffer from thirst or hunger;
no blistering heat or
anything else
will ever
torture you again

*Heaven
on earth
is
possible*

*Accept
all human beings
because in front
of God
everybody is equal*

Your
earthly happiness
is to yield
to the joy
of enlightenment

Forgive
the people
if they treat you
impolitely

Forgive
humanity;
this will open
their way
to God

Be a
freedom fighter
for the cause
of God

*Healing of the sick
and miracles
will
happen*

Be innovative

in

your

thinking

As you imagine,
so it
will be

Don't
worry
about
tomorrow

Let go of
old thinking patterns
and habits
and bid
them farewell

You
must be
born
again

God
works in you
and through
you

*Always
keep your goal
in mind,
which is love*

*There
is no greater love
than to give
your life
for your friends*

Leave
behind
your old life
and follow me

Words of Caution

Always remember that the gifts and talents given to you by God can be taken from you at any time.

The day of judgement can arrive when you least expect it.

Thank
the Lord daily
for
your talents

Proclaim God's coming

*Don't break
your head
trying to convert
the negative
into positive*

Set
impulses
and
let it happen

*Your focus
lies on
the
spiritual work*

Public
compulsory events
must be
avoided

*Incorporate
your energy without judging,
just by the will
of your
spiritual guidance*

Live deliberately
in
God's love

The love
of God
is the turning point
in everything
you do

Be there
for others
with
infinite patience

If need be,
remain uncomfortable
with assertiveness
and in love

Let go
of everything which pulls you back;
the only way
your life can take
a new course

Always
keep your energy high
and positive
and send love

You are here
as
God's instrument
for the needy

*Honour
your marriage,
children
and family*

Form
an unity
and collect
all forces

Just
work with
love

Love
thy
neighbour

It is necessary
that you endure
and
still remain silent

Stand firm and be incorruptible

Bow
to
God's
greatness

*Take
a firm stand
on
God's cause*

*Ask
and
you shall
receive*

Always
strive towards
God's
love

*Stand strong
in faith and
represent
your point*

Always
expect
to receive
your desires

*Let
God rule
and stop
controlling*

*God will reward
every person
according
to his deeds*

*Acknowledge
the uniqueness
of every
human being*

*Show backbone
and courage
and
let it happen*

Words of Encouragement

We receive all kinds of support, because hope does not disappoint us.

The Love of God is poured into our hearts through the Holy Spirit (according to Romans 5, 5).

According to St John's Book of Revelation our victory is certain because: "To the one who is victorious, I will give the right to sit with me on my throne, just as I was victorious and sat down with my Father on his throne".

(Rev 3, 21)

*You are
the light
and
the love*

Remain
vigilant
and stand firm
in faith

*Do not
be fainthearted but
resolute
and strong*

You may
hope
for
a better life

Your thoughts
will be
fulfilled
like wishes

Your persistence
in faith
will
pay off

Your will be
rewarded manifold
for your
unwavering trust

You are
a gift
from God
to humanity

*Your
decision-making
will be
strengthened*

Stay
on
your
path

God will
guide you
to only one goal,
which is love

The force of life
comes
from God
only

*You will be
rewarded
by God
for your efforts*

Your rewards
will be manifold
if you follow
the way of God

Words of Consolation

You are shining examples of integrity, straightness, honesty, trust and purity in thought and belief.

God
is your companion
on all
your ways

*All who belong
to God and serve Him,
will receive
His seal
of approval*

*Your sensitivity
is natural,
since you are
an angel*

*God's
mercy and love
have really come
to us*

All
secrets
will be
revealed

Your
mental strength
will be
worthwhile

Peace
to
this
house

You are
under
the highest
protection

Be an Angel on Earth
as best you can
then Earth will be your Heaven.

References

New International Version (NIV bible)
http://www.biblegateway.com/versions/New-International-
Version-NIV-Bible/

Prof. Dr. Günter Stemberger, Sr. Dr. Mirjam Prager OSB:
**„Die Bibel, Altes und Neues Testament,
Einheitsübersetzung",**
Augsburg, 1987, Weltbild-Verlag

Christa Keding-Pütz:
**„Gesund durch analytische Kinesiologie. Der Muskeltest als
Brücke zu ganzheitlicher Heilung",**
2007, Oesch Verlag AG, ISBN 9783035050196

Max Freedom Long:
**„Geheimes Wissen hinter Wundern. Die Entdeckung der
HUNA-Lehre",**
2006, Schirner, ISBN 3-89767-487-4

Otha Wingo:
**„ Das Huna Arbeitsbuch, Psychologische und praktische
Anwendung des Huna-Wissens",**
München, 1994, Knaur, ISBN 3-426-86062-7

Carlos Castaneda:
„Die Reise nach Ixtlan"
Frankfurt am Main, 2001, Fischer, ISBN 3-596-21809-8

Roberto, Assagioli:
**„ Die Schulung des Willens. Methoden der Psychotherapie
und der Selbsttherapie",**
Paderborn, 1982, Junfermann, ISBN 3-87387-202-1

Imprint

Contact person and author
Dorothea Westhofen-Kunz
Püttlingen, Germany
dorotheawk@stars-of-heaven.com
www.stars-of-heaven.com

Impulses
Dr Heike Winschiers-Theophilus
Windhoek, Namibia

Editorial
Angelica Bergmann
Windhoek, Namibia

Jenni Jacobs
Windhoek, Namibia

Paul Mooney
Johannesburg, South Africa

Cover, graphics and logo
Romo Sinkala
Windhoek, Namibia

Layout
Claudia Habenicht
Somerset West, South Africa

Production and Publisher
Books on Demand GmbH
Norderstedt, Germany

I am the Alpha and the Omega,

the beginning
and the end,

says the Lord God,

which is,
and which was,
and which is to come,

the Almighty.

(Revelation , 1, 8)